Buddha

Under the Bodhi Tree

By Stefan Czernecki

BAYEUX ARTS

CALGARY, CANADA

*I am deeply grateful to Michael Haijtink for assisting me
in the research and preparation of the manuscript
and for his assistance in the completion of the art work.*

For Griffin Buzzelle Rhodes,
my little teacher.

Published in 1998 by
Bayeux Arts, Inc.
119 Stratton Crescent, SW
Calgary, Canada T3H IT7

Visit our Website: www.bayeux.com

Designed by: Andrew Johnstone

Printed in Hong Kong

Canadian Cataloguing in Publication Data

Czernecki, Stefan, 1946-
Buddha under the bodhi tree

ISBN 1-896209-15-7 (bound)
ISBN 1-896209-19-X (paperback)

1. Gautama Buddha – Juvenile literature. 1. Title
BQ892.C93 1998   j294.3'63   C98-910690-X

*Bayeux Arts, Inc. gratefully acknowledges the support
of the Canada Council for the Arts
and the Alberta Foundation for the Arts
for our publishing programme.*

One night long ago in a small kingdom in the north of India where the whitest mountains touch the bluest sky Queen Maya, wife of King Suddhodana, had a dream. She dreamed of a white elephant carrying a lotus flower. It came down from the sky and said to her: "You will have a son."

Under a full moon which washed the earth in a flood of silver, a boy named Siddhartha was born. It was a time of great happiness.

One day a wise man from a distant forest came to the palace with a gift for the young prince. It was a beautiful fawn. The wise man said to the King; "This young prince will become a great teacher when he has seen the Four Signs: old age, sickness, death and a holy man".

Each day King Suddhodana watched Siddhartha play with the fawn in the royal gardens. The king was worried about the prophecy. "I want my son to inherit this great kingdom," he thought. "I will surround the little prince with beauty and luxury so he will never want to leave the palace."

Many years passed and the fawn had grown into a beautiful deer. One morning when Siddhartha went into the garden he found the deer lying under a tree. The deer had fallen ill.

"What has happened to you?" Siddhartha cried out. He sat down beside his friend and embraced him. But the deer died and Siddhartha, trembling, was overcome with grief.

"What if I too grow old, get sick and die?" he thought to himself.

"Even when I am king I cannot escape this fate?" Siddhartha became frightened.

He grew restless and unhappy. He no
longer cared for the beauty and luxury of
the palace and one day Siddhartha stepped
out into the world.

Outside the palace he saw a holy man sitting happily under a tree.

"How can you be so happy with all this unhappiness in the world?" Siddhartha asked.

"I have overcome fear and have found peace," the holy man said.

"I want to become a holy man like you and search for true happiness and a way to end pain and suffering," Siddhartha said.

The prophecy was fulfilled. Siddhartha
had seen the Four Signs.

He exchanged his beautiful silk clothes
for a monk's robe. Carrying an alms bowl,
Siddhartha set off on his journey.

In the mountains he met a group of hermits who had given up a life of comfort for a life of hardship. "Sit in the hot scorching sun. Sleep on a bed of stones. Eat only a single grain of rice a day and drink only raindrops that fall on your tongue. That is how you will find happiness," one of the hermits said.

Siddhartha sat with the hermits for many years. He became so thin his navel touched his backbone. But he did not find happiness.

Siddhartha took his bowl and went to a nearby village where he was offered a meal of rice and milk. When his strength had returned Siddhartha sat under a Bodhi tree. He said to himself: "I will not move until I have found the way to true happiness." Siddhartha then closed his eyes and began to meditate.

Dark clouds gathered above him. Mara,
the Evil One, had come to distract
Siddhartha from his search for happiness.

He tried to frighten him with thunder and
lightning. Siddhartha was not afraid.
Outraged, Mara disappeared, and a full
moon appeared from behind the dark clouds.

Siddhartha opened his eyes. He had overcome his fears and had found happiness. He was enlightened. He accepted that old age, sickness and death are the way of nature. Siddhartha had become a Buddha: the Awakened One.

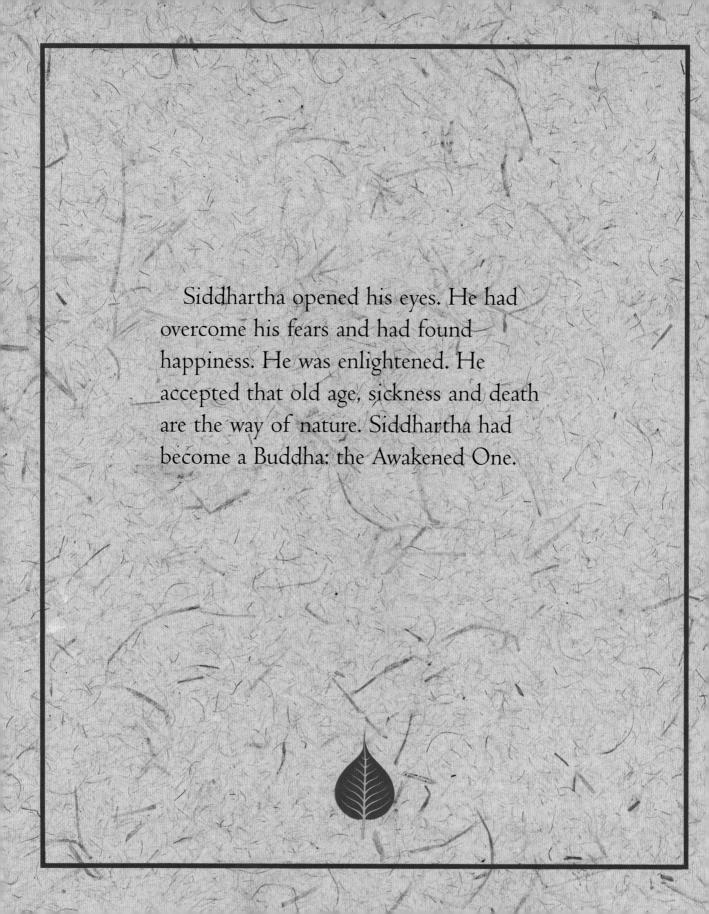

Siddhartha devoted the rest of his life teaching love and compassion for all living things and showing others the way to happiness.

One night under a full moon Siddhartha lay down to rest. He was old and had fallen ill. He did not fear his death as he closed his eyes for the last time. His journey had come to an end.

Buddha – Historical Information

Buddha was the title of Siddhartha Gautama, a religious leader who founded Buddhism and lived in India between, it is believed, 563 and 483 B.C. His father ruled a kingdom which lay to the north of the present day city of Varanasi, one of the holiest centres of Hinduism.

At the age of 29, Buddha renounced his princely status, all luxuries, and became an ascetic. Gradually, his life of asceticism and deep meditation brought him "the great enlightenment." He and his disciples spread Buddhism far and wide.